The Wiersbe
BIBLE STUDY SERIES

The Wiersbe
BIBLE STUDY SERIES

1 PETER

How to

Make the Best

of Times

Out of Your

Worst of Times

David C Cook®
transforming lives together

THE WIERSBE BIBLE STUDY SERIES: 1 PETER
Published by David C Cook
4050 Lee Vance Drive
Colorado Springs, CO 80918 U.S.A.

David C Cook U.K., Kingsway Communications
Eastbourne, East Sussex BN23 6NT, England

The graphic circle C logo is a registered trademark of David C Cook.

ISBN 978-1-4347-0375-0
eISBN 978-1-4347-0467-2

© 2011 Warren W. Wiersbe

The Team: Steve Parolini, Karen Lee-Thorp, Amy Konyndyk,
Nick Lee, Jack Campbell, Karen Athen
Series Cover Design: John Hamilton Design
Cover Photo: Veer (PHP3041020)

Printed in the United States of America
First Edition 2011

6 7 8 9 10 11 12 13 14 15

082317

Contents

Introduction to 1 Peter

From Trials to Hope

Peter wrote this letter to Christians who were going through various trials. The apostle knew that a severe "fiery trial" was just around the corner, and he wanted to prepare believers for it. After all, what life does to us depends on what life finds in us.

For the most part, Christians in the Western world have enjoyed comfortable lives. Our brothers and sisters behind iron and bamboo curtains have suffered for their faith. Now there is every indication that the time is approaching when it will cost us to take a stand for Christ. The only "comfortable" Christian will be a "compromising" Christian, and the believer's comfort will be costly.

Prepare, Don't Despair

Peter has given to us a precious letter that encourages us to hope in the Lord no matter how trying the times may be. Down through the centuries, the church has experienced various fiery trials, and yet Satan has not been able to destroy it. The church today is facing a fiery trial, and we must be prepared.

But, whatever may come, Peter is still saying to each of us: "Be hopeful!" The glory is soon to come!

—Warren W. Wiersbe

How to Use This Study

This study is designed for both individual and small-group use. We've divided it into eight lessons—each references one or more chapters in Warren W. Wiersbe's commentary *Be Hopeful* (second edition, David C Cook, 2009). While reading *Be Hopeful* is not a prerequisite for going through this study, the additional insights and background Wiersbe offers can greatly enhance your study experience.

The **Getting Started** questions at the beginning of each lesson offer you an opportunity to record your first thoughts and reactions to the study text. This is an important step in the study process as those "first impressions" often include clues about what it is your heart is longing to discover.

The bulk of the study is found in the **Going Deeper** questions. These dive into the Bible text and, along with helpful excerpts from Wiersbe's commentary, help you examine not only the original context and meaning of the verses but also modern application.

Looking Inward narrows the focus down to your personal story. These intimate questions can be a bit uncomfortable at times, but don't shy away from honesty here. This is where you are asked to stand before the mirror of God's Word and look closely at what you see. It's the place to take a good look at yourself in light of the lesson and search for ways in which you can grow in faith.

Going Forward is the place where you can commit to paper those things you want or need to do in order to better live out the discoveries you made in the Looking Inward section. Don't skip or skim through this. Take the time to really consider what practical steps you might take to move closer to Christ. Then share your thoughts with a trusted friend who can act as an encourager and accountability partner.

Finally, there is a brief **Seeking Help** section to close the lesson. This is a reminder for you to invite God into your spiritual-growth process. If you choose to write out a prayer in this section, come back to it as you work through the lesson and continue to seek the Holy Spirit's guidance as you discover God's will for your life.

Tips for Small Groups

A small group is a dynamic thing. One week it might seem like a group of close-knit friends. The next it might seem more like a group of uncomfortable strangers. A small-group leader's role is to read these subtle changes and adjust the tone of the discussion accordingly.

Small groups need to be safe places for people to talk openly. It is through shared wrestling with difficult life issues that some of the greatest personal growth is discovered. But in order for the group to feel safe, participants need to know it's okay *not* to share sometimes. Always invite honest disclosure, but never force someone to speak if he or she isn't comfortable doing so. (A savvy leader will follow up later with a group member who isn't comfortable sharing in a group setting to see if a one-on-one discussion is more appropriate.)

Have volunteers take turns reading excerpts from Scripture or from the commentary. The more each person is involved even in the mundane tasks, the more they'll feel comfortable opening up in more meaningful ways.

The leader should watch the clock and keep the discussion moving. Sometimes there may be more Going Deeper questions than your group can cover in your available time. If you've had a fruitful discussion, it's okay to move on without finishing everything. And if you think the group is getting bogged down on a question or has taken off on a tangent, you can simply say, "Let's go on to question 5." Be sure to save at least ten to fifteen minutes for the Going Forward questions.

Finally, soak your group meetings in prayer—before you begin, during as needed, and always at the end of your time together.

Born for Glory
(1 PETER 1:1–12; 5:12–14)

Before you begin …
- *Pray for the Holy Spirit to reveal truth and wisdom as you go through this lesson.*
- *Read 1 Peter 1:1–12; 5:12–14. This lesson references chapters 1 and 2 in* Be Hopeful. *It will be helpful for you to have your Bible and a copy of the commentary available as you work through this lesson.*

Getting Started

From the Commentary

The writer identified himself as "Peter, an apostle of Jesus Christ" (1 Peter 1:1). Some liberals have questioned whether a common fisherman could have penned this letter, especially since Peter and John were both called "unlearned and ignorant men" (Acts 4:13). However, this phrase only means "laymen without formal schooling"; that is, they were not professional religious leaders. We must never underestimate the training Peter had for three years with the Lord Jesus, nor should we minimize the work of the Holy Spirit in his life. Peter is a perfect illustration of the truth expressed in 1 Corinthians 1:26–31.

—*Be Hopeful,* pages 19–20

1. Is it important to know for certain that this letter was written by the disciple Peter? Why or why not? What clues do we have to suggest he was the author? What evidence is there that this might be in question? What role might the Holy Spirit have played in the creation of this letter? How does this answer the critics of Peter's authorship?

More to Consider: Peter's given name was Simon, but Jesus changed it to Peter (John 1:35–42). Why is this change significant?

2. Choose one verse or phrase from 1 Peter 1:1–12; 5:12–14 that stands out to you. This could be something you're intrigued by, something that makes you uncomfortable, something that puzzles you, something that resonates with you, or just something you want to examine further. Write that here.

Going Deeper

From the Commentary

Peter indicated that he wrote this letter "at Babylon" (1 Peter 5:13) where there was an assembly of believers. There is no evidence either from church history or tradition that Peter ministered in ancient Babylon which, at that time, did have a large community of Jews. There was another town called "Babylon" in Egypt, but we have no proof that Peter ever visited it. "Babylon" is probably another name for the city of Rome, and we do have reason to believe that Peter ministered in Rome and was probably martyred there. Rome is called "Babylon" in Revelation 17:5 and 18:10. It was not unusual for persecuted believers during those days to write or speak in "code."

In saying this, however, we must not assign more to Peter than is due him. He did *not* found the church in Rome nor serve as its first bishop. It was Paul's policy not to minister where any other apostle had gone (Rom. 15:20); so Paul would not have ministered in Rome had Peter arrived there first. Peter probably arrived in Rome after Paul was released from his first imprisonment, about the year AD 62. First Peter was written about the year 63. Paul was martyred about 64, and perhaps that same year, or shortly after, Peter laid down his life for Christ.

—*Be Hopeful,* page 21

3. Why is it important to know where Peter was when he wrote this letter? How might that have affected the tone or message of the letter? How do our circumstances influence what we share with others? How can God use our circumstances to make a positive difference in others?

From the Commentary

> Peter called the recipients of this letter "strangers" (1 Peter 1:1), which means "resident aliens, sojourners." They are called "strangers and pilgrims" in 1 Peter 2:11. These people were citizens of heaven through faith in Christ (Phil. 3:20), and therefore were not permanent residents on earth. Like Abraham, they had their eyes of faith centered on the future city of God (Heb. 11:8–16). They were in the world, but not of the world (John 17:16).
>
> —*Be Hopeful,* pages 21–22

4. In what ways were the early Christians "strangers" in their culture? In what ways are Christians today "strangers" in the world? What makes them stand out?

From the History Books

Around the time of Peter's letter, believers were becoming a "scattered" people as well as a "strange" people. The word translated "scattered" (*diaspora*) was a technical term for the Jews who lived outside of Palestine. The word has since been adopted by historians to refer to a variety of cultures and their dispersion from the place they once called home. Whatever the context or usage, a diaspora is always accompanied by a sense of displacement.

5. What fears might the early Christians have had about their dispersion into the larger world? What excitement might they have had about being spread far and wide? How do both of these issues relate to the church today (both the local church and the church in general)?

From the Commentary

First Peter is a letter of encouragement (1 Peter 5:12). We have noted that the theme of *suffering* runs throughout the letter, but so also does the theme *of glory* (see 1 Peter 1:7–8, 11, 21; 2:12; 4:11–16; 5:1, 4, 10–11). One of the encouragements that Peter gives suffering saints is the assurance that their suffering will one day be transformed into glory (1 Peter 1:6–7; 4:13–14; 5:10). This is possible only because the Savior suffered for us and then entered into His glory (1 Peter 1:11; 5:1). The sufferings of Christ are mentioned often in this letter (1 Peter 1:11; 3:18; 4:1, 13; 5:1).

—*Be Hopeful,* page 24

6. What are some examples of encouragement found in 1 Peter 1:1–12? Why is 1 Peter a letter of hope? What reasons for having courage in the midst of trials did Peter give in 1:6–9?

From the Commentary

Because of the death and resurrection of Jesus Christ, believers have been "begotten again" to a living hope, and that hope includes the glory of God. But, what do we mean by "the glory of God"?

The glory of God means the sum total of all that God is and does. "Glory" is not a separate attribute or characteristic of God, such as His holiness, wisdom, or mercy. Everything that God is and does is characterized by glory.

He is glorious in wisdom and power, so that everything He thinks and does is marked by glory. He reveals His glory in creation (Ps. 19), in His dealings with the people of Israel, and especially in His plan of salvation for lost sinners.

When we were born the first time, we were not born for glory. "For all flesh is as grass, and all the glory of man as the flower of grass" (1 Peter 1:24, quoted from Isa. 40:6). Whatever feeble glory man has will eventually fade and disappear, but the glory of the Lord is eternal. The works of man done for the glory of God will last and be rewarded (1 John 2:17). But the selfish human achievements of sinners will one day vanish to be seen no more. One reason that we have encyclopedias and the Internet is so that we can learn about the famous people who are now forgotten!

—*Be Hopeful*, page 30

7. How do our lives reveal God's glory? What does it mean to be chosen by the Father (1 Peter 1:2) to participate in God's glory? (See Eph. 1:3–4; Rom. 11:33–36.) What should our response be to this truth?

From the Commentary

A Christian's hope is *a living hope* because it is grounded on the living Word of God (1 Peter 1:23) and was made possible by the living Son of God who arose from the dead. A "living hope" is one that has life in it and therefore can give life to us. Because it has life, it grows and becomes greater and more beautiful as time goes on. Time destroys most hopes; they fade and then die. But the passing of time only makes a Christian's hope that much more glorious.

Peter called this hope *an inheritance* (1 Peter 1:4). As the children of the King, we share His inheritance in glory (Rom. 8:17–18; Eph. 1:9–12). We are included in Christ's last will and testament, and we share the glory with Him (John 17:22–24).

—*Be Hopeful*, page 32

8. How does 1 Peter 1:3–4 describe a believer's hope? What is a "living hope"? How is the inheritance God offers unlike any earthly inheritance?

More to Consider: Trials are not easy. Peter didn't suggest that we take a careless attitude toward trials, because that would be deceitful. Trials produce what he called "heaviness" (1 Peter 1:6 KJV). The word means "to experience grief or pain." Read Matthew 26:37 and 1 Thessalonians 4:13. What do these verses teach us about trials?

From the Commentary

Not only is the glory being "reserved" for us, but we are being kept for the glory! In my travels, I have sometimes gone to a hotel or motel, only to discover that the reservations have been confused or cancelled. This will not happen to us when we arrive in heaven, for our future home and inheritance are guaranteed and reserved.

"But suppose *we* don't make it?" a timid saint might ask. But we will; for all believers are being "kept by the power of God." The word translated "kept" is a military word that means "guarded, shielded." The tense of the verb reveals that we are *constantly* being guarded by God, assuring us that we shall safely arrive in heaven. This same word is used to describe the soldiers guarding Damascus when Paul made his escape (2 Cor. 11:32). See also Jude 24–25 and Romans 8:28–39.

—*Be Hopeful,* pages 32–33

9. Why is it important to understand that our future home and inheritance are guaranteed? How does that affect the way we live our lives today? In what ways are believers "kept by the power of God"?

From the Commentary

The Christian philosophy of life is not "pie in the sky by and by." It carries with it a *present* dynamic that can turn suffering into glory *today*. Peter gave four directions for enjoying the glory now, even in the midst of trials.

(1) Love Christ (1 Peter 1:8). Our love for Christ is not based on physical sight, because we have not seen Him. It is based on our spiritual relationship with Him and what the Word has taught us about Him.

(2) Trust Christ (v. 8). We must live by faith and not by sight.

(3) Rejoice in Christ (v. 8). You may not be able to rejoice *over* the circumstances, but you can rejoice *in* them by centering your heart and mind on Jesus Christ.

(4) Receive from Christ (vv. 8–12). "Believing ...

receiving" is God's way of meeting our needs. If we love Him, trust Him, and rejoice in Him, then we can receive from Him all that we need to turn trials into triumphs.

—*Be Hopeful,* pages 36–37

10. Review 1 Peter 1:8–12. What does it mean to live by faith and not by sight? How do we do that? How do all our circumstances (whether good or bad) teach us something about Jesus?

Looking Inward

Take a moment to reflect on all that you've explored thus far in this study of 1 Peter 1:1–12; 5:12–14. Review your notes and answers and think about how each of these things matters in your life today.

Tips for Small Groups: To get the most out of this section, form pairs or trios and have group members take turns answering these questions. Be honest and as open as you can in this discussion, but most of all, be encouraging and supportive of others. Be sensitive to those who are going through particularly difficult times and don't press for people to speak if they're uncomfortable doing so.

11. Have you ever felt that sense of "displacement" that the early Christians must have felt as they were dispersed to many nations? What was it like for you? What prompted that feeling? How did it affect the way you lived out your faith?

12. Where do you find hope in your life? What are some areas of life where you could use more hope? How will you seek that out?

13. What does it mean to you that you have already received your inheritance from God? What does that look like in daily life? What are you most looking forward to about the inheritance to come? How can Peter's letter give you hope?

Going Forward

14. Think of one or two things that you have learned that you'd like to work on in the coming week. Remember that this is all about quality, not quantity. It's better to work on one specific area of life and do it well than to work on many and do poorly (or to be so overwhelmed that you simply don't try).

Do you need to develop hope that is more solid than just positive thinking? Do you need to offer hope to others? Be specific. Go back through 1 Peter 1:1–12; 5:12–14 and put a star next to the phrase or verse that is most encouraging to you. Consider memorizing this verse.

Real-Life Application Ideas: Peter's message was one of hope for a people who felt like "strangers in a strange land." Think of people you know who may feel out of sorts or anxious about their circumstances. These could be friends or relatives or coworkers or missionaries or soldiers. Then contact these people (a traditional letter will speak loudest) and offer them encouraging words. Be a hope bringer to them.

Seeking Help

15. Write a prayer below (or simply pray one in silence), inviting God to work on your mind and heart in those areas you've noted above. Be honest about your desires and fears.

Notes for Small Groups:
- *Look for ways to put into practice the things you wrote in the Going Forward section. Talk with other group members about your ideas and commit to being accountable to one another.*
- *During the coming week, ask the Holy Spirit to continue to reveal truth to you from what you've read and studied.*
- *Before you start the next lesson, read 1 Peter 1:13–21. For more in-depth lesson preparation, read chapter 3, "Staying Clean in a Polluted World," in* Be Hopeful.

Holiness
(1 PETER 1:13–21)

Before you begin ...
- *Pray for the Holy Spirit to reveal truth and wisdom as you go through this lesson.*
- *Read 1 Peter 1:13–21. This lesson references chapter 3 in* Be Hopeful. *It will be helpful for you to have your Bible and a copy of the commentary available as you work through this lesson.*

Getting Started

From the Commentary

In the first section of 1 Peter 1, Peter emphasized *walking in hope,* but now his emphasis is *walking in holiness.* The two go together, for "every man that hath this hope in him purifieth himself, even as he is pure" (1 John 3:3).
—*Be Hopeful,* page 43

1. What is holiness? What does it mean to walk in holiness? How do hope and holiness go together?

More to Consider: The root meaning of the word translated "holy" is "different." How does this help us understand what it means to be holy? (See 1 Peter 4:4.)

2. Choose one verse or phrase from 1 Peter 1:13–21 that stands out to you. This could be something you're intrigued by, something that makes you uncomfortable, something that puzzles you, something that resonates with you, or just something you want to examine further. Write that here.

Going Deeper

From the Commentary

"The revelation of Jesus Christ" (1:13) is another expression for the "living hope" and "the appearing of Jesus Christ." Christians live in the future tense; their present actions and decisions are governed by this future hope. Just as an engaged couple makes all their plans in the light of that future wedding, so Christians today live with the expectation of seeing Jesus Christ.

"Gird up the loins of your mind" simply means, "Pull your thoughts together! Have a disciplined mind!" The image is that of a robed man, tucking his skirts under the belt, so he can be free to run.

—*Be Hopeful,* page 44

3. What does it mean to have a disciplined mind? How do Christians develop disciplined minds?

From the Commentary

A Christian who is looking for the glory of God has a greater motivation for present obedience than a Christian who ignores the Lord's return. The contrast is illustrated in the lives of Abraham and Lot (Gen. 12–13; Heb. 11:8–16). Abraham had his eyes of faith on that heavenly city, so he had no interest in the world's real estate. But Lot, who had tasted the pleasures of the world in Egypt, gradually moved toward Sodom. Abraham brought blessing to his home, but Lot brought judgment. Outlook determined outcome.

Not only should we have a disciplined mind, but we should also have a *sober* mind. The word means "to be calm, steady, controlled; to weigh matters." Unfortunately some people get "carried away" with prophetic studies and lose their spiritual balance. The fact that Christ is coming should encourage us to be calm and collected (1 Peter 4:7). The fact that Satan is on the prowl is another reason to be sober-minded (1 Peter 5:8). Anyone whose mind becomes undisciplined, and whose life "falls apart" because of prophetic studies, is giving evidence that he does not really understand Bible prophecy.

We should also have an *optimistic* mind. "Hope to the end" means "set your hope fully." Have a hopeful outlook! A friend of mine sent me a note one day that read: "When the *outlook* is gloomy, try the *uplook!*" Good advice, indeed! It has to be dark for the stars to appear.

—*Be Hopeful,* pages 44–45

4. In what ways does the phrase "outlook determines outcome; attitude determines action" apply to Peter's message? What does it look like in practical terms to be sober-minded? What is the result of a God-focused mind-set?

From Today's World

Even the most optimistic idealist would have to agree that modern society's view of "right and wrong" has undergone a radical shift from black and white to shades of gray. While conservative views remain among subcultures (including much of Christianity), the world's view continues to broaden, often under the auspices of inclusiveness and tolerance. While both of these concepts have positive implications (and are, in some contexts, even biblical), they also tend to lead to a cultural acceptance of questionable morality.

5. What has changed over the past few decades that has led to a broader understanding of what is morally acceptable? How do these changes affect the church and how it functions? What additional challenges for pursuing holiness do today's believers face in light of our changing societal norms?

From the Commentary

Children inherit the nature of their parents. God is holy; therefore, as His children, we should live holy lives. We are "partakers of the divine nature" (2 Peter 1:4) and ought to reveal that nature in godly living.

Peter reminded his readers of what they were before they trusted Christ. They had been *children of disobedience* (Eph. 2:1–3), but now they were to be obedient children. True salvation always results in obedience (Rom. 1:5; 1 Peter 1:2). They had also been *imitators of the world,* "fashioning themselves" after the standards and pleasures of the world. Romans 12:2 translates this same word as "conformed to this world." Unsaved people tell us that they want to be "free and different," yet they all imitate one another!

The cause of all this is *ignorance* that leads to *indulgence.* Unsaved people lack spiritual intelligence, and this causes them to give themselves to all kinds of fleshly and worldly indulgences (see Acts 17:30; Eph. 4:17ff.). Since we were born with a fallen nature, it was natural for us to live sinful lives. Nature determines appetites and actions. A dog and a cat behave differently because they have different natures.

—*Be Hopeful,* pages 45–46

6. Review 1 Peter 1:14–15. Why does Peter connect "evil desires" with ignorance? What is his warning to believers about these desires? What does

it look like to "be holy in all you do"? How is this contrasted with the fallen nature?

From the Commentary

"It is written!" is a statement that carries great authority for the believer. Our Lord used the Word of God to defeat Satan, and so may we (Matt. 4:1–11; see Eph. 6:17). But the Word of God is not only a sword for battle, it is also a light to guide us in this dark world (Ps. 119:105; 2 Peter 1:19), food that strengthens us (Matt. 4:4; 1 Peter 2:2), and water that washes us (Eph. 5:25–27).

—*Be Hopeful,* page 47

7. What is the role of the Word of God in the lives of dedicated believers? (See John 17:17.) How do we enjoy the benefits of God's Word? (See Ps. 1:1–3.) How do we entrust our entire lives to God's Word?

More to Consider: Peter quoted from the book of Leviticus, "Ye shall be holy; for I am holy" (11:44 KJV). Does this mean that the Old Testament law is authoritative today for New Testament Christians? Explain.

From the Commentary

As God's children, we need to be serious about sin and about holy living. Our heavenly Father is a holy (John 17:11) and righteous Father (John 17:25). He will not compromise with sin. He is merciful and forgiving, but He is also a loving disciplinarian who cannot permit His children to enjoy sin. After all, it was sin that sent His Son to the cross. If we call God "Father," then we should reflect His nature.

—*Be Hopeful,* page 48

8. What is the judgment Peter wrote about in 1:17? (See also Rom. 5:1–10; 8:1–4; Col. 2:13; 1 Peter 2:24; Heb. 10:10–18.) Why do you think Peter included this message in his letter? How is this message applicable to us today?

From the Commentary

> The love of God is the highest motive for holy living. In
> 1:18–21, Peter reminded his readers of their salvation
> experience, a reminder that all of us regularly need. This
> is one reason our Lord established the Lord's Supper, so
> that regularly His people would remember that He died
> for them.
>
> —*Be Hopeful*, page 50

9. What reminders did Peter give the believers in 1:17–21? What do these
reminders imply about the audience Peter was writing to? Why are these
important reminders for believers? How are we reminded of these things
today?

From the Commentary

> Peter was a witness of Christ's sufferings (1 Peter 5:1) and
> mentioned His sacrificial death often in this letter (1 Peter
> 2:21ff; 3:18; 4:1, 13; 5:1). In calling Christ "a lamb," Peter
> was reminding his readers of an Old Testament teaching

that was important in the early church, and that ought to be important to us today. It is the doctrine of substitution: an innocent victim giving his life for the guilty.

—*Be Hopeful,* page 51

10. Review the origins of the doctrine of sacrifice in Genesis 3; 22:13; Exodus 12; John 1:29. In what ways did Peter speak to the significance of this doctrine? Why is it important to note that this sacrifice was ordained before the creation of the world?

Looking Inward

Take a moment to reflect on all that you've explored thus far in this study of 1 Peter 1:13–21. Review your notes and answers and think about how each of these things matters in your life today.

Tips for Small Groups: To get the most out of this section, form pairs or trios and have group members take turns answering these questions. Be honest and as open as you can in this discussion, but most of all, be encouraging and supportive of others. Be sensitive to those who are going through particularly difficult times and don't press for people to speak if they're uncomfortable doing so.

11. What does it mean to you to be "holy"? What are some of the practical things you do to seek a life of holiness? What are some of the obstacles you face?

12. Peter talks of being sober-minded and spiritually minded. How do you accomplish this in your own life? Are there areas of your life where you need to focus more on spiritual things? How will you do this?

13. In what ways were you ignorant before you knew Christ? How did that influence your behavior? Your attitudes? How does faith in Christ change those behaviors and attitudes?

Going Forward

14. Think of one or two things that you have learned that you'd like to work on in the coming week. Remember that this is all about quality, not quantity. It's better to work on one specific area of life and do it well than to work on many and do poorly (or to be so overwhelmed that you simply don't try).

Do you need to be more spiritually minded? Be specific. Go back through 1 Peter 1:13–21 and put a star next to the phrase or verse that is most encouraging to you. Consider memorizing this verse.

Real-Life Application Ideas: Peter cautions believers to stop conforming to the evil desires they once had before knowing Christ. Take a few minutes to consider some of the choices, habits, and attitudes you have today that don't honor your relationship with Christ. Spend time in prayer, asking God to help you deal with these issues. If possible, speak with a close, trusted leader about the things you're struggling with and work together on a plan to attack these through prayer, study, and discipline.

Seeking Help

15. Write a prayer below (or simply pray one in silence), inviting God to work on your mind and heart in those areas you've noted above. Be honest about your desires and fears.

Notes for Small Groups:

- *Look for ways to put into practice the things you wrote in the Going Forward section. Talk with other group members about your ideas and commit to being accountable to one another.*

- *During the coming week, ask the Holy Spirit to continue to reveal truth to you from what you've read and studied.*

- *Before you start the next lesson, read 1 Peter 1:22— 2:10. For more in-depth lesson preparation, read chapter 4, "Christian Togetherness," in* Be Hopeful.

Togetherness
(1 PETER 1:22—2:10)

Before you begin ...
- *Pray for the Holy Spirit to reveal truth and wisdom as you go through this lesson.*
- *Read 1 Peter 1:22—2:10. This lesson references chapter 4 in* Be Hopeful. *It will be helpful for you to have your Bible and a copy of the commentary available as you work through this lesson.*

Getting Started

From the Commentary

One of the painful facts of life is that the people of God do not always get along with each other. You would think that those who walk in *hope* and *holiness* would be able to walk in *harmony,* but this is not always true. From God's divine point of view, there is only one body (see Eph. 4:4–6), but what we see with human eyes is a church divided and sometimes at war. There is today a desperate need for spiritual unity.

—*Be Hopeful,* page 55

1. How did Peter emphasize spiritual unity in 1 Peter 1:22—2:10? Why was spiritual unity so important to Peter? Why is it important to the church today?

2. Choose one verse or phrase from 1 Peter 1:22—2:10 that stands out to you. This could be something you're intrigued by, something that makes you uncomfortable, something that puzzles you, something that resonates with you, or just something you want to examine further. Write that here.

Going Deeper

From the Commentary

> The only way to enter God's spiritual family is by a spiritual birth, through faith in Jesus Christ (John 3:1–16). Just as there are two parents in physical birth, so there

are two parents in spiritual birth: the Spirit of God (John 3:5–6) and the Word of God (1 Peter 1:23). The new birth gives to us a new nature (2 Peter 1:4) as well as a new and living hope (1 Peter 1:3).

—*Be Hopeful,* page 55

3. What does it mean to be spiritually reborn? What does the new nature look like when compared to the old nature? How does hope figure into the new nature?

More to Consider: Review the story of the Tower of Babel in Genesis 11. How is this an example of how human works decay? How does this relate to the message in 1 Peter 1:23–25?

From the Commentary

Peter used two different words for love: *philadelphia,* which is "brotherly love," and *agape,* which is godlike sacrificial love. It is important that we share both kinds of love. We share brotherly love because we are brothers and sisters in Christ and have likenesses. We share *agape* love because we belong to God and therefore can overlook differences.

—*Be Hopeful,* page 56

4. How can you tell the difference between sincere love (whether brotherly or sacrificial) and manufactured love? Why did it take God's intervention to give us true love? How is our love for others evidence that we have been born of God? (See 1 John 4:7–21.)

From Today's World

The word *love* has been used to describe everything from a favorite food to the sort of sacrificial love Peter talked about in his letter. In popular media, the word might refer to sex one minute and friendship the next. Sometimes it's used sincerely, sometimes sarcastically. But rarely does the word mean the same thing from one usage to the next. Because of our culture's obsession with the word, its meaning has been both stretched and diluted.

5. Why is our culture obsessed by the idea of love? How does popular culture's usage of the word affect the way believers use it? How can believers redeem the word and its meaning in our culture today?

From the Commentary

> The love that we share with each other, and with a lost world, must be generated by the Spirit of God. It is a *constant* power in our lives, and not something that we turn on and off like a radio.
>
> Not only is this love a spiritual love, but it is also a *sincere* love ("unfeigned"). We love "with a pure heart." Our motive is not to get but to give. There is a kind of "success psychology" popular today that enables a person to subtly manipulate others in order to get what he wants. If our love is sincere and from a pure heart, we could never "use people" for our own advantage.
>
> This love is also a *fervent* love, and this is an athletic term that means "striving with all of one's energy." Love is something we have to work at, just as an Olympic contestant has to work at his particular skills. Christian love

is not a feeling; it is a matter of the will. We show love to others when we treat them the same way God treats us. God forgives us, so we forgive others. God is kind to us, so we are kind to others. It is not a matter of *feeling* but of *willing,* and this is something we must constantly work at if we are to succeed.

—*Be Hopeful,* page 57

6. Respond to this statement: "The love that we share with each other, and with a lost world, must be generated by the Spirit of God." How did Peter attest to this? How do the Word of God and the Spirit of God help us love one another?

From the Commentary

God's Word *has* life, *gives* life, and *nourishes* life. We should have appetites for the Word, just like hungry newborn babes! We should want the *pure* Word, unadulterated, because this alone can help us grow. When I was a child, I did not like to drink milk (and my father worked for the Borden Dairy!), so my mother used to add various

syrups and powders to make my milk tastier. None of
them really ever worked. It is sad when Christians have
no appetite for God's Word, but must be "fed" religious
entertainment instead. As we grow, we discover that
the Word is milk for babes, but also strong meat for the
mature (1 Cor. 3:1–4; Heb. 5:11–14). It is also bread
(Matt. 4:4) and honey (Ps. 119:103).

—*Be Hopeful,* pages 57–58

7. Review 1 Peter 2:1–3. What keeps believers from having an appropriate
"appetite"? How did Peter address this issue? What is the difference
between Christians who are growing in the Word and those who are not?

From the Commentary

There is only one Savior, Jesus Christ, and only one
spiritual building, the church. Jesus Christ is the chief
cornerstone of the church (Eph. 2:20), binding the building together. Whether we agree with each other or not,
all true Christians belong to each other as stones in God's
building.

Peter gave a full description of Jesus Christ, the stone. He is a *living* stone because He was raised from the dead in victory. He is the *chosen* stone of the Father, and He is *precious.* Peter quoted Isaiah 28:16 and Psalm 118:22 in his description and pointed out that Jesus Christ, though chosen by God, was rejected by men. He was not the kind of Messiah they were expecting, so they stumbled over Him. Jesus referred to this same Scripture when He debated with the Jewish leaders (Matt. 21:42ff.; see Ps. 118:22). Though rejected by men, Jesus Christ was exalted by God!

—*Be Hopeful,* pages 58–59

8. What was the root cause of the Jewish stumbling? (See 1 Peter 2:8.) Why do you think Peter uses the stone metaphor to describe both Jesus and the stumbling block? How does this contrast help to teach believers about Jesus' role in their lives?

More to Consider: When Solomon built his temple, his workmen followed the plans so carefully that everything fit together on the construction site (1 Kings 6:7). How is living the life God has given us like following a blueprint? Where do believers find this blueprint?

From the Commentary

We are a "holy priesthood" and a "royal priesthood." This corresponds to the heavenly priesthood of our Lord, for He is both King and Priest (see Heb. 7). In the Old Testament no king in Israel served as a priest; and the one king who tried was judged by God (2 Chron. 26:16–21). Our Lord's heavenly throne is a throne of grace from which we may obtain by faith all that we need to live for Him and serve Him (Heb. 4:14–16).

In the Old Testament period, God's people *had* a priesthood, but today, God's people *are* a priesthood. Each individual believer has the privilege of coming into the presence of God (Heb. 10:19–25). We do not come to God through any person on earth, but only through the one Mediator, Jesus Christ (1 Tim. 2:1–8). Because He is alive in glory, interceding for us, we can minister as holy priests.

—*Be Hopeful,* page 60

9. What does it mean that we are a "holy priesthood"? How should this affect the way we live our lives? In what ways is it a privilege to serve as a priest?

From the Commentary

The description of the church in 1 Peter 2:9–10 paral-
lels God's description of Israel in Exodus 19:5–6 and
Deuteronomy 7:6. In contrast to the disobedient and
rebellious nation of Israel, God's people today are His
chosen and holy nation. This does not suggest that God
is through with Israel, for I believe He will fulfill His
promises and His covenants and establish the promised
kingdom. But it does mean that the church today is to
God and the world what Israel was meant to be.

We are a *chosen generation,* which immediately speaks of
the grace of God. God did not choose Israel because they
were a great people, but because He loved them (Deut.
7:7–8). God has chosen us purely because of His love and
grace. "You did not choose me, but I chose you" (John
15:16 NIV).

We are the *people of God.* In our unsaved condition, we
were not God's people, because we belonged to Satan and
the world (Eph. 2:1–3, 11–19). Now that we have trusted
Christ, we are a part of God's people. We are a people of
his own special possession, because He purchased us with
the blood of His own Son (Acts 20:28).

—Be Hopeful, page 62

10. In what ways are believers today "a holy nation"? (See Phil. 3:20.) What
was the darkness we were called out of? What does it mean, in practical
terms, that together we are the people of God?

Looking Inward

Take a moment to reflect on all that you've explored thus far in this study of 1 Peter 1:22—2:10. Review your notes and answers and think about how each of these things matters in your life today.

> *Tips for Small Groups: To get the most out of this section, form pairs or trios and have group members take turns answering these questions. Be honest and as open as you can in this discussion, but most of all, be encouraging and supportive of others. Be sensitive to those who are going through particularly difficult times and don't press for people to speak if they're uncomfortable doing so.*

11. What does it mean to you that you were "reborn" spiritually? How is this truth evident in your own life? In what ways do you still struggle with the old life?

12. What are ways you live out brotherly love (*philadelphia*) and sacrificial love (*agape*)? How does your relationship with Christ help you love in these ways? When have you felt loved in these ways?

13. To what extent do you live as part of God's holy nation, and to what extent do you tend to live your Christian life on your own? What do you have to contribute to the people of God? What do you need from them?

Going Forward

14. Think of one or two things that you have learned that you'd like to work on in the coming week. Remember that this is all about quality, not quantity. It's better to work on one specific area of life and do it well than to work on many and do poorly (or to be so overwhelmed that you simply don't try).

Do you want to love certain people in your life more sacrificially? Be specific. Go back through 1 Peter 1:22—2:10 and put a star next to the phrase or verse that is most encouraging to you. Consider memorizing this verse.

Real-Life Application Ideas: Consider how your church lives out the truth that God's people are a "holy nation." Meet with your small group and discuss what this means in terms of church work. How can a congregation be holy in practice? Work together to come up with practical ideas for living out holiness in your community.

Seeking Help

15. Write a prayer below (or simply pray one in silence), inviting God to work on your mind and heart in those areas you've noted above. Be honest about your desires and fears.

Notes for Small Groups:

- *Look for ways to put into practice the things you wrote in the Going Forward section. Talk with other group members about your ideas and commit to being accountable to one another.*

- *During the coming week, ask the Holy Spirit to continue to reveal truth to you from what you've read and studied.*

- *Before you start the next lesson, read 1 Peter 2:11–25. For more in-depth lesson preparation, read chapter 5, "Somebody's Watching You!" in* Be Hopeful.

4/5/19

Pray for Community group
Debbie
Pray for Barbara's friend –
Pray for Jan's children / step children
Pray for health for all
Pray for Laurie's family + friends
Pray for Carol's son whose marriage is
breaking up

4/5/19

4/11
4/25 — Kathy
5/9 — me
5/23 ~ ?

Lesson 4

Submission

(1 PETER 2:11–25)

Before you begin ...
- *Pray for the Holy Spirit to reveal truth and wisdom as you go through this lesson.*
- *Read 1 Peter 2:11–25. This lesson references chapter 5 in Be Hopeful. It will be helpful for you to have your Bible and a copy of the commentary available as you work through this lesson.*

Getting Started

From the Commentary

The central section of Peter's letter (1 Peter 2:11—3:12) emphasizes *submission* in the life of a believer. This is certainly not a popular topic in this day of lawlessness and the quest for "personal fulfillment," but it is an important one. Peter applied the theme of submission to the life of a believer as a citizen (1 Peter 2:11–17), a worker (1 Peter 2:18–25), a marriage partner (1 Peter

3:1–7), and a member of the Christian assembly (1 Peter
3:8–12).

—*Be Hopeful,* page 67

1. Why is submission a sticky subject for believers? What misguided
interpretations of this concept have made it so controversial?

2. Choose one verse or phrase from 1 Peter 2:11–25 that stands out to you.
This could be something you're intrigued by, something that makes you
uncomfortable, something that puzzles you, something that resonates with
you, or just something you want to examine further. Write that here.

Going Deeper

From the Commentary

> As Christians, we must constantly remind ourselves *who we are;* and Peter did this in 1 Peter 2:11. To begin with, we are *God's dearly beloved children.* Eight times in his two epistles, Peter reminded his readers of God's love for them (1 Peter 2:11; 4:12; 2 Peter 1:7; 3:1, 8, 14–15, 17). In ourselves, there is nothing that God can love, but He loves us because of Jesus Christ. "This is my beloved Son, in whom I am well pleased" (2 Peter 1:17). Because of our faith in Jesus Christ, we are "accepted in the beloved" (Eph. 1:6).
>
> —*Be Hopeful,* page 68

3. Review 1 Peter 2:11–12. What are some habitual sins that can plague people who doubt they are "dearly beloved" (2:11 KJV)? In what ways does our love relationship with Jesus motivate us to live godly lives? (See John 14:15, 23.)

From the Commentary

Not only are we God's beloved children, but we are also "strangers [sojourners] and pilgrims" in this world.

We are also *soldiers involved in a spiritual battle.*

Most of all, we are *witnesses to the lost around us.* The word *Gentiles* here has nothing to do with race, since it is a synonym for "unsaved people" (1 Cor. 5:1; 12:2; 3 John 7). Unsaved people are watching us, speaking against us (1 Peter 3:16; 4:4), and looking for excuses to reject the gospel.

—*Be Hopeful,* page 68

4. What does it mean to live an "honest" life (1 Peter 2:12 KJV)? How would Peter define this? How can the church be the model for honest or honorable living? Why is this important?

From Today's World

The mission field today is a little different than it was a hundred years ago. While there are still plenty of opportunities for American Christians to go overseas and reach out to peoples who don't know what it means to follow Christ, the landscape has changed a bit (thanks to global connectivity afforded by the Internet age). People now have access to just about any information they could want—including facts and stories, fiction and truth about what it means to be a believer.

5. How has the Internet age affected mission fields today? How can it help believers reach out to nonbelievers? What challenges does it set before us as we try to live in ways that will bring others to glorify God? How might Peter's message in 1 Peter 2:11–12 be applied to our Internet age?

From the Commentary

Peter encouraged his readers to bear witness to the lost, by word and deed, so that one day God might visit them and save them. "The day of visitation" could mean that day when Christ returns and every tongue will confess that He is Lord. But I think the "visitation" Peter mentioned here is the time when God visits lost sinners and saves them by His grace. The word is used in this sense in Luke 19:44. When these people do trust Christ, they will

glorify God and give thanks because we were faithful to
witness to them even when they made life difficult for us.

—*Be Hopeful,* page 69

6. What does it mean to bear witness to the lost by word and deed? How
might God use this witness to prepare people for His grace? What does this
tell us about listening to God, being open to His direction?

ended cession

4/16/19

From the Commentary

Of course, *everything* we do should be for the glory of the
Lord and the good of His kingdom! But Peter was careful
to point out that Christians in society are representa-
tives of Jesus Christ. It is our responsibility to "advertise
God's virtues" (1 Peter 2:9, author's translation). This is
especially true when it comes to our relationship to government and people in authority.

As Christian citizens, we should submit to the authority
vested in human government. The word translated "ordi-
nance" in the King James Version simply means "creation
or institution." It does not refer to each individual law,

but to the institutions that make and enforce the laws. It is possible to submit to the institutions and still disobey the laws.

—*Be Hopeful,* page 70

7. Read Daniel 1. How was the way Daniel and his friends refused to obey the king's dietary regulations an example of honoring the king and respecting the authorities? What does it look like to honor our authorities today? Is this always easy? Why or why not?

[handwritten notes]

From the Commentary

Peter named the offices we are to respect. "The king" meant "the emperor." In democratic nations, we have a president or premier. Peter did not criticize the Roman government or suggest that it be overthrown. God's church has been able to live and grow in all kinds of political systems. The "governors" are those under the supreme authority who administer the laws and execute justice. Ideally, they should punish those who do evil and praise those who do good. This ideal was not always reached in Peter's day (see Acts 24:24–27), nor is it reached in our own. Again, we must remind ourselves to respect the office even if we cannot respect the officer.

—Be Hopeful, pages 71–72

8. How do you think treating those in authority with respect helped Christians in Peter's day gain a hearing for the gospel in their culture? How does "doing good" silence ignorant people? How can we relate to the government today in ways that gain credibility for the gospel?

More to Consider: As Christians, we must exercise discernment in our relationship to human government. Paul was willing to suffer personally in Philippi (Acts 16:16–24), but he was unwilling to sneak out of town like a criminal (vv. 35–40). When Paul was arrested on false charges, he used his citizenship to protect himself (22:22–29) and to insist on a fair trial before Caesar (25:1–12). How can Christians discern what's right and wrong relating to authorities in today's society?

From the Commentary

> Peter addressed the Christian slaves in the congregations, and again he stressed the importance of submission. Some newly converted slaves thought that their spiritual freedom also guaranteed personal and political freedom, and they created problems for themselves and the churches. Paul dealt with this problem in 1 Corinthians 7:20–24, and also touched on it in his letter to his friend Philemon. The gospel eventually overthrew the Roman Empire and the terrible institution of slavery, even though the early church did not preach against either one.
>
> —*Be Hopeful*, page 73

9. Review 1 Peter 2:18–25. How does what Peter said about slaves apply to employees today? Is it a direct correlation? Why or why not? What are the takeaways from this message?

From the Commentary

Peter encouraged these suffering slaves by presenting three "pictures" of Jesus Christ.

(1) He is our Example in His life (1 Peter 2:21–23). All that Jesus did on earth, as recorded in the four gospels, is a perfect example for us to follow. But He is especially our example in the way He responded to suffering.

(2) He is our Substitute in His death (v. 24). He died as the sinner's Substitute. This entire section reflects that great "Servant Chapter," Isaiah 53, especially Isaiah 53:5–7, but also verses 9 and 12. Jesus did not die as a martyr; He died as a Savior, a sinless Substitute.

(3) He is our Watchful Shepherd in heaven (v. 25). In the Old Testament, the sheep died for the shepherd, but at Calvary, the Shepherd died for the sheep (John 10).

—Be Hopeful, pages 74–76

10. Who are the people in today's society that suffer and long for encouragement? How is Peter's description of Jesus encouragement for those who suffer?

Looking Inward

Take a moment to reflect on all that you've explored thus far in this study of 1 Peter 2:11–25. Review your notes and answers and think about how each of these things matters in your life today.

> *Tips for Small Groups: To get the most out of this section, form pairs or trios and have group members take turns answering these questions. Be honest and as open as you can in this discussion, but most of all, be encouraging and supportive of others. Be sensitive to those who are going through particularly difficult times and don't press for people to speak if they're uncomfortable doing so.*

11. What is the first thing that comes to mind when you hear the word *submission?* How does that affect the way you view this biblical concept? What about submission appeals to you? What troubles you?

12. How are you bearing witness to the lost through words and deeds? What are some ways you could do this better?

13. Who are the authorities you must honor in your life? What challenges do you face as you attempt to honor them as Peter taught? How have you failed to honor authorities? How have you succeeded even when you've disagreed with them?

Going Forward

14. Think of one or two things that you have learned that you'd like to work on in the coming week. Remember that this is all about quality, not quantity. It's better to work on one specific area of life and do it well than to work on many and do poorly (or to be so overwhelmed that you simply don't try).

Do you need to practice biblical submission in a particular relationship or arena? Be specific. Go back through 1 Peter 2:11–25 and put a star next to the phrase or verse that is most encouraging to you. Consider memorizing this verse.

> *Real-Life Application Ideas: Consider all the places where you must submit to authority (work, church, home, community). Are there areas where you are prone to challenge the authority rather than offer it due respect? Ask God for wisdom in dealing with those circumstances, and where appropriate, talk with the authority to resolve any remaining animosity or dissonance.*

Seeking Help

15. Write a prayer below (or simply pray one in silence), inviting God to work on your mind and heart in those areas you've noted above. Be honest about your desires and fears.

Notes for Small Groups:

- *Look for ways to put into practice the things you wrote in the Going Forward section. Talk with other group members about your ideas and commit to being accountable to one another.*

- *During the coming week, ask the Holy Spirit to continue to reveal truth to you from what you've read and studied.*

- *Before you start the next lesson, read 1 Peter 3:1–17. For more in-depth lesson preparation, read chapters 6 and 7, "Wedlock or Deadlock?" and "Preparing for the Best!" in* Be Hopeful.

1 Peter 2:2↓
1 Peter 3:↓7 ↑ to 17

Love and Blessings

(1 PETER 3:1–17)

Before you begin …
- *Pray for the Holy Spirit to reveal truth and wisdom as you go through this lesson.*
- *Read 1 Peter 3:1–17. This lesson references chapters 6 and 7 in* Be Hopeful. *It will be helpful for you to have your Bible and a copy of the commentary available as you work through this lesson.*

Getting Started

From the Commentary

The phrases "in the same manner" and "in like manner" refer us back to Peter's discussion of the example of Jesus Christ (1 Peter 2:21–25). Just as Jesus was submissive and obedient to God's will, so a Christian husband and wife should follow His example.

Much of our learning in life comes by way of imitation. Grandparents have a delightful time watching their grandchildren pick up new skills and words as they grow up. If we imitate the best models, we will become better people and better achievers, but if we imitate the wrong models, it will cripple our lives and possibly ruin our characters. The role models that we follow influence us in every area of life.

—*Be Hopeful,* pages 79–80

1. Review 1 Peter 3:1, 7. How is an understanding of Christlikeness critical to building a good marriage? What does it mean to submit "in the same way"?

More to Consider: Peter pointed to Sarah as a model for Christian wives to follow. Why would Peter choose Sarah as a role model? What qualities did she have that line up with what Peter was teaching? What are some of the things that might have raised a few eyebrows upon her mention? What was it about Sarah that granted her a mention in Hebrews 11 (KJV)?

2. Choose one verse or phrase from 1 Peter 3:1–17 that stands out to you. This could be something you're intrigued by, something that makes you uncomfortable, something that puzzles you, something that resonates with you, or just something you want to examine further. Write that here.

Going Deeper

From the Commentary

> In 1 Peter 3:1–6, Peter twice reminded Christian wives that they were to be submissive to their husbands (1 Peter 3:1, 5). The word translated "subjection" is a military term that means "to place under rank." God has a place for everything; He has ordained various levels of authority (see 1 Peter 2:13–14). He has ordained that the husband be the head of the home (Eph. 5:21ff.) and that, as he submits to Christ, his wife should submit to him. Headship is not dictatorship, but the loving exercise of divine authority under the lordship of Jesus Christ.
>
> —*Be Hopeful,* page 81

3. What reasons did Peter give in 3:1–6 for why a wife should submit to her husband? What does it mean for the husband to be the head of the home?

From the Commentary

> Why did Peter devote more space to instructing the wives than the husbands? Because the Christian wives were experiencing a whole new situation and needed guidance. In general, women were kept down in the Roman Empire, and their new freedom in Christ created new problems and challenges. Furthermore, many of them had unsaved husbands and needed extra encouragement and enlightenment.
>
> —*Be Hopeful,* pages 84–85

4. What advice did Peter give to husbands in 3:7? How does this correspond to the advice he gave wives? What marriage advice can we glean from this single verse? In what ways is this advice applicable to relationships in general?

From Today's World

Turn on the TV and flip through the channels and you're sure to encounter a wide variety of relationships—from traditional married couples to single parents to gay couples and everything in between. The same is true in movies and other media. Just a few decades ago, a show depicting two people living together who weren't husband and wife would have been considered shocking. Our shifting culture is no more vividly evident than as portrayed in popular media.

5. Do television shows and movies accurately portray relationships as they are in the real world today? Explain. Why do you think there's such a push to stretch the definition of marriage? What would Peter have to say about the world's definition of what's okay and what's not when it comes to relationships?

From the Commentary

We have noted that love is a recurring theme in Peter's letters, not only God's love for us, but also our love for others. Peter had to learn this important lesson himself, and he had a hard time learning it! How patient Jesus had to be with him!

We should begin with *love for God's people* (1 Peter 3:8). The word *finally* means "to sum it all up." Just as the whole of the law is summed up in love (Rom. 13:8–10), so the whole of human relationships is fulfilled in love. This applies to every Christian and to every area of life.

—*Be Hopeful,* pages 91–92

6. What is the difference between like-mindedness (or unity of mind, see Phil. 2:1–11) and uniformity? How can Christians find unity even though they are diverse?

From the Commentary

Not only should we love God's people, but we should also *love our enemies* (1 Peter 3:9). The recipients of this letter were experiencing a certain amount of personal persecution because they were doing the will of God. Peter warned them that *official* persecution was just around the corner, so they had better prepare. The church today had better prepare, because difficult times are ahead.

As Christians, we can live on one of three levels. We can return evil for good, which is the satanic level. We can return good for good and evil for evil, which is the human level. Or, we can return good for evil, which is the divine level. Jesus is the perfect example of this latter approach (1 Peter 2:21–23). As God's loving children, we must do more than give "an eye for an eye, and a tooth for a tooth" (Matt. 5:38–48), which is the basis *for justice.* We must operate on the basis of *mercy,* for that is the way God deals with us.

—Be Hopeful, pages 92–93

7. What are the challenges that can make it hard to love our enemies? What advice did Peter give for how to do this?

From the Commentary

Peter quoted Isaiah 8:13–14 to back up his admonition that the fear of the Lord conquers every other fear: "But in your hearts set apart Christ as Lord" (1 Peter 3:15 NIV).

The setting of the Isaiah quotation is significant. Ahaz, King of Judah, faced a crisis because of an impending invasion by the Assyrian army. The kings of Israel and Syria wanted Ahaz to join them in an alliance, but Ahaz refused, so Israel and Syria threatened to invade Judah! Behind the scenes, Ahaz confederated himself with Assyria! The prophet Isaiah warned him against ungodly alliances and urged him to trust God for deliverance. "Sanctify the Lord of hosts [armies] himself; and let him be your fear, and let him be your dread" (Isa. 8:13).

—*Be Hopeful,* pages 95–96

8. Review 1 Peter 3:13–15. How do our fears lead to wrong decisions? What does it mean to fear God? How can the fear of the Lord help us deal with other fears?

More to Consider: The word happy *in 1 Peter 3:14 (KJV; blessed in NIV) is the same as* blessed *in Matthew 5:10–12. Why do you think Peter used this word here? What does it tell us about Peter's understanding of Jesus' teaching in Matthew?*

From the Commentary

Our word "conscience" comes from two Latin words: *con,* meaning "with," and *scio,* meaning "to know." The conscience is that internal judge that witnesses to us, that enables us to "know with," either approving our actions or accusing (see Rom. 2:14–15). Conscience may be compared to a window that lets in the light of God's truth. If we persist in disobeying, the window gets dirtier and dirtier, until the light cannot enter. This leads to a "defiled conscience" (Titus 1:15). A "seared conscience" is one that has been so sinned against that it no longer is sensitive to what is right and wrong (1 Tim. 4:2). It is even possible for the conscience to be so poisoned that it approves things that are bad and accuses when the person does good! This the Bible calls "an evil conscience" (Heb. 10:22). A criminal feels guilty if he "squeals" on his friends, but happy if he succeeds in his crime!

—*Be Hopeful,* page 97

9. In what ways does "conscience" depend on knowledge? How does studying God's Word affect our conscience and therefore our sensitivity to right and wrong?

From the Commentary

Peter made it clear that conscience *alone* is not the test of what is right or wrong. A person can be involved in either "well-doing" or "evildoing." For a person to disobey God's Word and claim it is right simply because his conscience does not convict him, is to admit that something is radically wrong with his conscience. Conscience is a safe guide only when the Word of God is the teacher.

More and more, Christians in today's society are going to be accused and lied about. Our personal standards are not those of the unsaved world. As a rule, Christians do not *create* problems; they *reveal* them. Let a born-again person start to work in an office or move into a college dormitory, and in a short time there will be problems. Christians are lights in this dark world (Phil. 2:15), and they reveal "the unfruitful works of darkness" (Eph. 5:11).

—Be Hopeful, pages 98–99

10. What are some ways the early Christians suffered for doing good? How do believers experience this today?

Looking Inward

Take a moment to reflect on all that you've explored thus far in this study of 1 Peter 3:1–17. Review your notes and answers and think about how each of these things matters in your life today.

Tips for Small Groups: To get the most out of this section, form pairs or trios and have group members take turns answering these questions. Be honest and as open as you can in this discussion, but most of all, be encouraging and supportive of others. Be sensitive to those who are going through particularly difficult times and don't press for people to speak if they're uncomfortable doing so.

11. If you're married, how do you relate to Peter's advice to husbands and wives? If you're not, what can you glean from this advice to improve your relationships with those you love? What is the hardest piece of Peter's marriage advice? Do you agree with all of it? If not, explain.

12. What is most challenging to you about the command to love your enemies? Describe a time when you were successful at this. Describe a time when you failed. How do God's Word and God's Spirit help you to love those who are difficult to love?

13. What does it mean to you to fear God? What fears do you have a hard time trusting God with? What role does faith play in fearing God? In trusting God with your earthly fears?

Going Forward

14. Think of one or two things that you have learned that you'd like to work on in the coming week. Remember that this is all about quality, not quantity. It's better to work on one specific area of life and do it well than to work on many and do poorly (or to be so overwhelmed that you simply don't try).

Do you want to do good to someone who has treated you badly? Be specific. Go back through 1 Peter 3:1–17 and put a star next to the phrase or verse that is most encouraging to you. Consider memorizing this verse.

Real-Life Application Ideas: If you're married, consider attending a marriage retreat that teaches biblical principles of love. Come prepared to honestly examine what it means to be in submission or to cherish. Use the retreat time to look for ways to grow your relationship according to biblical principles. If you're not married but hope to be someday, spend time with like-minded friends studying these principles and looking for truths that can be applied to your life now and in the future.

Seeking Help

15. Write a prayer below (or simply pray one in silence), inviting God to work on your mind and heart in those areas you've noted above. Be honest about your desires and fears.

Notes for Small Groups:

- *Look for ways to put into practice the things you wrote in the Going Forward section. Talk with other group members about your ideas and commit to being accountable to one another.*

- *During the coming week, ask the Holy Spirit to continue to reveal truth to you from what you've read and studied.*

- *Before you start the next lesson, read 1 Peter 3:18–22. For more in-depth lesson preparation, read chapter 8, "Learning from Noah," in* Be Hopeful.

Lessons from Noah

(1 PETER 3:18–22)

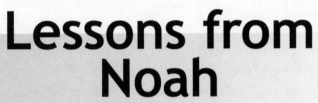

Before you begin ...
- *Pray for the Holy Spirit to reveal truth and wisdom as you go through this lesson.*
- *Read 1 Peter 3:18–22. This lesson references chapter 8 in* Be Hopeful. *It will be helpful for you to have your Bible and a copy of the commentary available as you work through this lesson.*

Getting Started

From the Commentary

When Peter wrote this section of his letter, he had no idea that it would be classified as one of the most difficult portions of the New Testament. Good and godly interpreters have wrestled with these verses, debated and disagreed, and have not always left behind a great deal of spiritual help. We may not be able to solve all the problems found in this section, but we do want to get the practical help that Peter gave to encourage Christians in difficult days.

—*Be Hopeful,* page 103

1. What makes 1 Peter 3:18–22 such a difficult passage to understand? Why do students of Scripture have such a divided opinion on its meaning? What was your initial conclusion after reading this section?

More to Consider: In his second letter, Peter wrote that some of what Paul said was "hard to understand" (2 Peter 3:14–16). How might this also apply to Peter's own message in 1 Peter 3:18–22?

2. Choose one verse or phrase from 1 Peter 3:18–22 that stands out to you. This could be something you're intrigued by, something that makes you uncomfortable, something that puzzles you, something that resonates with you, or just something you want to examine further. Write that here.

Going Deeper

From the Commentary

Everything else in this section is incidental to what Peter had to say about Jesus Christ. This material is parallel to what Peter wrote in 1 Peter 2:21ff. Peter presented Jesus Christ as the perfect example of one who suffered unjustly, and yet obeyed God.

In 1 Peter 3:17, Peter wrote about suffering for well-doing rather than for evildoing, and then he gave the example of Jesus Christ. Jesus was the "Just One" (Acts 3:14), and yet He was treated unjustly. Why? That He might die for the unjust ones and bring them to God! He died as a substitute (1 Peter 2:24), and He died only once (Heb. 9:24–28).

The phrase "bring us to God" is a technical term that means "gain audience at court." Because of the work of Christ on the cross, we now have an open access to God.

—Be Hopeful, pages 103–4

3. In what ways did Jesus suffer for "well-doing" as opposed to wrongdoing? Why does the cross give us open access to God? (See Rom. 5:1–2; Eph. 2:18; 3:12.) What does this access look like? (See Rom. 5:2; Heb. 10:19–23.)

From the Commentary

The phrase "made alive by the Spirit" creates a problem for us. In the Greek manuscripts, there were no capital letters; so we have no authority to write "Spirit" rather than "spirit." Greek scholars tell us that the end of 1 Peter 3:18 should read, "Being put to death with reference to the flesh, but made alive with reference to the spirit." The contrast is between flesh and spirit, as in Matthew 26:41 and Romans 1:3–4, and not between Christ's flesh and the Holy Spirit.

Our Lord had a real body (Matt. 26:26), soul (John 12:27), and spirit (Luke 23:46). He was not God inhabiting a man; He was the true God-Man. When He died, He yielded His spirit to the Father (Luke 23:46; see James 2:26). However, it seems evident that, if He was "made alive in the spirit," at some point His spirit must have died. It was probably when He was made sin for us and was forsaken by the Father (Mark 15:34; 2 Cor. 5:21). The phrase "quickened by [with reference to] the Spirit" (1 Peter 3:18) cannot mean resurrection, because resurrection has to do with *the body*.

So on the cross, our Lord suffered and died. His body was put to death, and His spirit died when He was made sin. But His spirit was made alive and He yielded it to the Father. Then according to Peter, sometime between His death and His resurrection Jesus made a special proclamation to "the spirits in prison."

—*Be Hopeful*, pages 104–5

4. Review 1 Peter 3:19–20. What is significant about the "spirits in prison" that Jesus visited? What did He proclaim to them? Why was that important to the early church (Peter's audience)? To us today?

From the Commentary

> Since death comes when the spirit leaves the body (James 2:26), then resurrection involves the spirit *returning* to the body (Luke 8:55). The Father raised Jesus from the dead (Rom. 6:4; 8:11), but the Son also had authority to raise Himself (John 10:17–18). It was a miracle! It is because of His resurrection that Christians have the "living hope" (1 Peter 1:3–4 NIV). We shall see later how the resurrection of Christ relates to the experience of Noah.
>
> —*Be Hopeful,* page 106

5. Review 1 Peter 3:21. What are the dangers of minimizing the importance of Jesus' resurrection? (See Rom. 1:4; 1 Thess. 4:13–18; Rev. 1:17–18.) What does the risen Christ provide for us that we need on a daily basis? (See Gal. 2:20.)

From the Commentary

> Forty days after His resurrection, our Lord ascended to heaven to sit at the right hand of the Father, the place of exaltation (Ps. 110:1; Acts 2:34–36; Phil. 2:5–11; Heb. 12:1–3). Believers are seated with Him in the heavenlies (Eph. 2:4–6), and through Him we are able to "reign in life" (Rom. 5:17). He is ministering to the church as High Priest (Heb. 4:14–16; 7:25) and Advocate (1 John 1:9–2:2). He is preparing a place for His people (John 14:1–6) and will one day come to receive them to Himself.
>
> *—Be Hopeful,* page 106

6. Why is it important that Christ's victory was over all "angels and authorities and powers" (1 Peter 3:22)? To whom does this refer? (See Eph. 6:10–12; Col. 2:15.) What does it mean for Christians to fight *from* victory instead of *for* it?

From the Commentary

The patriarch Noah was held in very high regard among Jewish people in Peter's day, and also among Christians. He was linked with Daniel and Job, two great men, in Ezekiel 14:19–20, and there are many references to the flood in both the Psalms and the Prophets. Jesus referred to Noah in His prophetic sermon (Matt. 24:37–39; see Luke 17:26–27), and Peter mentioned him in his second letter (2 Peter 2:5; see 3:6). He is named with the heroes of faith in Hebrews 11:7.

—*Be Hopeful,* page 107

7. What relationship did Peter see between the readers of his letter and the ministry of Noah? (See 2 Peter 2:5–9.) What circumstances might his readers have been experiencing that were similar to Noah's? How is this true for Christians today, too?

From the Commentary

> When Peter wrote that Noah and his family were "saved by water," he was careful to explain that this illustration does not imply salvation by baptism. Baptism is a "figure" of that which does save us, namely, "the resurrection of Jesus Christ" (1 Peter 3:21). Water on the body, or the body placed in water, cannot remove the stains of sin. Only the blood of Jesus Christ can do that (1 John 1:7—2:2). However, baptism does save us from one thing: a bad conscience. Peter had already told his readers that a good conscience was important to a successful witness (see 1 Peter 3:16), and a part of that "good conscience" is being faithful to our commitment to Christ as expressed in baptism.
>
> —*Be Hopeful,* page 108

8. How does baptism save us from a bad conscience? How is water baptism a good picture of what the Spirit does for us when we're saved? What's the connection between baptism and Christ's resurrection?

From the Commentary

It is easy to agree on the main lessons Peter was sharing with his readers, lessons that we need today.

First of all, *Christians must expect opposition.* As the coming of Christ draws near, our well-doing will incite the anger and attacks of godless people.

A second lesson is that *Christians must serve God by faith and not trust in results.* Noah served God and kept only seven people from the flood, yet God honored him.

Third, *we can be encouraged because we are identified with Christ's victory.* This is pictured in baptism, and the doctrine is explained in Romans 6. It is the baptism of the Spirit that identifies a believer with Christ (1 Cor. 12:12–13), and this is pictured in water baptism.

—*Be Hopeful,* pages 109–10

9. What sort of persecution should Christians expect today? What does it look like to live by faith and not trust in results? How does being identified with Christ because of baptism give us encouragement?

From the Commentary

> *Our baptism is important.* It identifies us with Christ and
> gives witness that we have broken with the old life and
> will, by His help, live a new life. The act of baptism is
> a pledge to God that we shall obey Him. To use Peter's
> illustration, we are agreeing to the terms of the contract.
> To take baptism lightly is to sin against God. Some people
> make too much of baptism by teaching that it is a means
> of salvation, while others minimize it. Both are wrong. If
> a believer is to have a good conscience, he must obey God.
>
> —*Be Hopeful,* page 110

10. Read 1 Peter 4:1–4. How does our baptism give witness that we've
broken with the old life? Why is it wrong to make baptism a test of
fellowship or spirituality?

Looking Inward

Take a moment to reflect on all that you've explored thus far in this study
of 1 Peter 3:18–22. Review your notes and answers and think about how
each of these things matters in your life today.

Tips for Small Groups: To get the most out of this section, form pairs or trios and have group members take turns answering these questions. Be honest and as open as you can in this discussion, but most of all, be encouraging and supportive of others. Be sensitive to those who are going through particularly difficult times and don't press for people to speak if they're uncomfortable doing so.

11. What's your reaction when you encounter Scripture passages that are difficult to understand? What frustrations do you have? How can you grow through these experiences?

12. What does the fact of Jesus' resurrection mean to you? How does this truth influence the way you live out your faith?

13. What is your experience with baptism? What role does it play in your faith story? In what ways is it an important symbol to you?

Going Forward

14. Think of one or two things that you have learned that you'd like to work on in the coming week. Remember that this is all about quality, not quantity. It's better to work on one specific area of life and do it well than to work on many and do poorly (or to be so overwhelmed that you simply don't try).

Do you want to deepen your awareness of Christ's resurrection? Do you want to live out the meaning of your baptism? Be specific. Go back through 1 Peter 3:18–22 and put a star next to the phrase or verse that is most encouraging to you. Consider memorizing this verse.

Real-Life Application Ideas: One of the key themes in this section of Peter's letter is the matter of baptism. If you've never been baptized, consider what that might mean to you. Talk with a pastor about your church's approach to baptism before you make your decision. If you have been baptized, this still might be a good opportunity to learn more about your church's baptism theology. Talk about this with small-group members and family members as you seek to better understand this important symbol and how it can inspire and encourage believers.

Seeking Help

15. Write a prayer below (or simply pray one in silence), inviting God to work on your mind and heart in those areas you've noted above. Be honest about your desires and fears.

Notes for Small Groups:

- *Look for ways to put into practice the things you wrote in the Going Forward section. Talk with other group members about your ideas and commit to being accountable to one another.*

- *During the coming week, ask the Holy Spirit to continue to reveal truth to you from what you've read and studied.*

- *Before you start the next lesson, read 1 Peter 4. For more in-depth lesson preparation, read chapters 9 and 10, "The Rest of Your Time" and "Facts about Furnaces," in* Be Hopeful.

Time and Trials
(1 PETER 4)

Before you begin …
- *Pray for the Holy Spirit to reveal truth and wisdom as you go through this lesson.*
- *Read 1 Peter 4. This lesson references chapters 9 and 10 in* Be Hopeful. *It will be helpful for you to have your Bible and a copy of the commentary available as you work through this lesson.*

Getting Started

From the Commentary

Peter had a great deal to say about *time.* Certainly the awareness of his own impending martyrdom had something to do with this emphasis (John 21:15–19; 2 Peter 1:12ff.). If a person really believes in eternity, then he will make the best use of time. If we are convinced that Jesus is coming, then we will want to live prepared lives.

Whether Jesus comes first or death comes first, we want
to make "the rest of the time" count for eternity.

—*Be Hopeful,* page 115

1. Read what Peter had to say about time. (See 1 Peter 1:5, 11, 17, 20; 4:2–3, 17; 5:6.) Why does believing in eternity encourage us to make the most of our time? What does it mean to make time count as a believer?

2. Choose one verse or phrase from 1 Peter 4 that stands out to you. This could be something you're intrigued by, something that makes you uncomfortable, something that puzzles you, something that resonates with you, or just something you want to examine further. Write that here.

Going Deeper

From the Commentary

Our Lord came to earth to deal with sin and to conquer it forever. He dealt with the ignorance of sin by teaching the truth and by living it before men's eyes. He dealt with the consequences of sin by healing and forgiving, and, on the cross, He dealt the final deathblow to sin itself. He was armed, as it were, with a militant attitude toward sin, even though He had great compassion for lost sinners.

Our goal in life is to "cease from sin." We will not reach this goal until we die or are called home when the Lord returns, but this should not keep us from striving (1 John 2:28—3:9). Peter did not say that suffering *of itself* would cause a person to stop sinning. Pharaoh in Egypt went through great suffering in the plagues, and yet he sinned even more! I have visited suffering people who cursed God and grew more and more bitter because of their pain.

—*Be Hopeful,* pages 116–17

3. According to Peter, how can suffering, in addition to Christ, help us have victory over sin? How does being identified with Christ's suffering give us victory over sin?

More to Consider: There are times when looking back at your life would be wrong, because Satan could use those memories to discourage you. But Peter looked back (see 1 Peter 4:3). Read Deuteronomy 5:15 and 1 Timothy 1:12–14 for two more examples of when looking back is a good thing. What do all these verses tell you about good reasons for looking back on your life? How can doing so help you?

From the Commentary

Unsaved people do not understand the radical change that their friends experience when they trust Christ and become children of God. They do not think it strange when people wreck their bodies, destroy their homes, and ruin their lives by running from one sin to another! But let a drunkard become sober, or an immoral person pure, and the family thinks he has lost his mind! Festus told Paul, "You are out of your mind!" (Acts 26:24 NASB), and people even thought the same thing of our Lord (Mark 3:21).

—Be Hopeful, page 118

4. Review 1 Peter 4:4–6. Why do conversions to Christianity surprise nonbelievers? What is so puzzling to them about such a change? What does this tell us about how we should relate to nonbelievers?

From the Commentary

Christians in the early church expected Jesus to return in their lifetime (Rom. 13:12; 1 John 2:18). The fact that He did not return does not invalidate His promise (2 Peter 3; Rev. 22:20). No matter what interpretation we give to the prophetic Scriptures, we must all live in expectancy. The important thing is that we shall see the Lord one day and stand before Him. How we live and serve today will determine how we are judged and rewarded on that day.

This attitude of expectancy must not turn us into lazy dreamers (2 Thess. 3:6ff.) or zealous fanatics. Peter gave "ten commandments" (1 Peter 4:7–19) to his readers to keep them in balance as far as the Lord's return was concerned:

1. Be sober-minded—v. 7

2. Watch unto prayer—v. 7

3. Have fervent love—v. 8

4. Use hospitality—v. 9

5. Minister your spiritual gifts—vv. 10–11

6. Think it not strange—v. 12

7. Rejoice—v. 13

8. Do not be ashamed—vv. 15–16

9. Glorify God—vv. 16–18

10. Commit yourself to God—v. 19

Often we hear of sincere people who go "off balance" because of an unbiblical emphasis on prophecy or a misinterpretation of prophecy. There are people who set dates for Christ's return, contrary to His warning (Matt. 25:13; see Acts 1:6–8); or they claim to know the name of the beast of Revelation 13. I have books in my library, written by sincere and godly men, in which all sorts of claims are made, only to the embarrassment of the writers.

—*Be Hopeful,* pages 119–20

5. What does it mean to be alert and of a sober mind (1 Peter 4:7 KJV)? How do believers live in expectancy, yet not knowing when Christ will return? How does living in expectancy change the way we relate to nonbelievers?

From the Commentary

If we really look for the return of Christ, then we shall think of others and properly relate to them. Love for the saints is important "above [before] all things." Love is the badge of a believer in this world (John 13:34–35).

Especially in times of testing and persecution, Christians need to love one another and be united in heart.

This love should be "fervent." The word pictures an athlete straining to reach the goal. It speaks of eagerness and intensity. Christian love is something we have to work at just the way an athlete works on his skills. It is not a matter of emotional feeling, though that is included, but of dedicated will. Christian love means that we treat others the way God treats us, obeying His commandments in the Word. It is even possible to love people that we do not like!

—*Be Hopeful,* page 122

6. Review 1 Peter 4:8–11. What does it look like to "love each other deeply"? Read Proverbs 10:12 (from which Peter quotes). What does this proverb teach us about Christian love? (See also James 5:20; 1 Cor. 13:4, 7.)

From the Commentary

Persecution is not something that is alien to the Christian life. Throughout history the people of God have suffered at the hands of the unbelieving world. Christians are different from unbelievers (2 Cor. 6:14–18), and this different kind of life produces a different kind of lifestyle. Much of what goes on in the world depends on lies, pride, pleasure, and the desire to "get more." A dedicated Christian builds his life on truth, humility, holiness, and the desire to glorify God.

This conflict is illustrated throughout the Bible. Cain was a religious man, yet he hated his brother and killed him (Gen. 4:1–8). The world does not persecute "religious people," but it does persecute righteous people. Why Cain killed Abel is explained in 1 John 3:12: "Because his own works were evil, and his brother's righteous." The Pharisees and Jewish leaders were religious people, yet they crucified Christ and persecuted the early church. "But beware of men," Jesus warned His disciples, "for they will deliver you up to the councils, and they will scourge you in their synagogues" (Matt. 10:17). Imagine scourging the servants of God in the very house of God!

—*Be Hopeful,* pages 129–30

7. Why might Christians in Peter's day (and even today) have been surprised when encountering trials? How does glorifying God invite persecution? What was Peter's encouragement to those who are suffering?

From the Commentary

> Literally, Peter wrote, "Be constantly rejoicing!" In fact, he mentioned joy in one form or another *four times* in 1 Peter 4:13–14! "Rejoice … be glad also with exceeding joy.… Happy are ye!" The world cannot understand how difficult circumstances can produce exceeding joy, because the world has never experienced the grace of God (see 2 Cor. 8:1–5).
>
> —*Be Hopeful,* pages 131–33

8. What are the privileges that accompany suffering? (See 1 Peter 4:13–14.) How does suffering bring us the ministry of the Holy Spirit? How does it enable us to glorify Jesus' name?

From the Commentary

> In the furnace of persecution and suffering, we often have more light by which we can examine our lives and ministries. The fiery trial is a refining process, by which God removes the dross and purifies us. One day, a fiery judgment will overtake the whole world (2 Peter 3:7–16).

Meanwhile, God's judgment begins at the house of God, the church (1 Peter 2:5). This truth ought to motivate us to be as pure and obedient as possible (see Ezek. 9 for an Old Testament illustration of this truth).

—*Be Hopeful,* page 134

9. How does persecution help us examine our lives? What questions should we ask as we examine our lives? For example, "Why am I suffering?" (See 1 Peter 4:15–16.)

From the Commentary

When we are suffering in the will of God, we can commit ourselves into the care of God. Everything else that we do as Christians depends on this. The word is a banking term; it means "to deposit for safekeeping" (see 2 Tim. 1:12). Of course, when you deposit your life in God's bank, you always receive eternal dividends on your investment.

This picture reminds us that we are valuable to God. He made us, redeemed us, lives in us, guards, and protects us. I saw a savings and loan association advertisement in the newspaper, reaffirming the financial stability of the firm and the backing of the Federal Deposit Insurance Corporation. In days of financial unsteadiness, such assurances are necessary to depositors. But when you "deposit" your life with God, you have nothing to fear, for He is able to keep you.

—Be Hopeful, page 136

10. What is the difference between simply suffering and suffering in the will of God? In what ways is a commitment to God more than a single action?

Looking Inward

Take a moment to reflect on all that you've explored thus far in this study of 1 Peter 4. Review your notes and answers and think about how each of these things matters in your life today.

Tips for Small Groups: To get the most out of this section, form pairs or trios and have group members take turns answering these questions. Be honest and as open as you can in this discussion, but most of all, be encouraging and supportive of others. Be sensitive to those who are going through particularly difficult times and don't press for people to speak if they're uncomfortable doing so.

11. Have you ever had non-Christians puzzle over your beliefs? What was that like? How did you respond to their surprise or confusion? What role does patience play in your encounters with nonbelievers?

12. What are some of the "fiery ordeals" you've faced? How has persecution helped you to grow? How has it challenged your faith? What have you learned from seasons or moments of persecution?

13. What does commitment to God look like to you? In what ways is it more than one action? What are the ongoing actions you take to commit to God?

Going Forward

14. Think of one or two things that you have learned that you'd like to work on in the coming week. Remember that this is all about quality, not quantity. It's better to work on one specific area of life and do it well than to work on many and do poorly (or to be so overwhelmed that you simply don't try).

Do you need to learn how to be strong when feeling persecuted? Be specific. Go back through 1 Peter 4 and put a star next to the phrase or verse that is most encouraging to you. Consider memorizing this verse.

Real-Life Application Ideas: Make a plan this week to spend time with nonbelievers, learning about their lives, listening to their concerns. If it feels appropriate, share the important elements of your story. Don't forget to talk about the faith aspects. But as Peter would warn, don't be surprised if they don't understand your beliefs. Be loving and kind and patient with them, and pray that God will use you to reveal His truth to them.

Seeking Help

15. Write a prayer below (or simply pray one in silence), inviting God to work on your mind and heart in those areas you've noted above. Be honest about your desires and fears.

Notes for Small Groups:
- *Look for ways to put into practice the things you wrote in the Going Forward section. Talk with other group members about your ideas and commit to being accountable to one another.*
- *During the coming week, ask the Holy Spirit to continue to reveal truth to you from what you've read and studied.*
- *Before you start the next lesson, read 1 Peter 5. For more in-depth lesson preparation, read chapters 11 and 12, "How to Be a Good Shepherd" and "From Grace to Glory!" in* Be Hopeful.

last mtg 4/23/19

A Good Shepherd
(1 PETER 5)

Susan m June 6/9
dinner 6:00 t

Before you begin …

- *Pray for the Holy Spirit to reveal truth and wisdom as you go through this lesson.*
- *Read 1 Peter 5. This lesson references chapters 11 and 12 in* Be Hopeful. *It will be helpful for you to have your Bible and a copy of the commentary available as you work through this lesson.*

Getting Started

From the Commentary

> Peter did not introduce himself in this letter as an apostle or a great spiritual leader, but simply as another elder. However, he did mention the fact that he had personally witnessed Christ's sufferings (see Matt. 26:36ff.). The Greek word translated "witness" gives us our English word *martyr*. We think of a martyr only as one who gives his life for Christ, and Peter did that, but basically,

person killed for his belief –

111

a martyr is a witness who tells what he has seen and heard.

—Be Hopeful, page 142

1. How does knowing Peter witnessed Jesus' suffering affect the message of 1 Peter 5? Why does his first-person perspective give the readers of his letter (including us today) something more than what a third-person account would provide?

More to Consider: Read 1 Peter 5:3. How is this warning like that in Luke 22:24–30? Why did Peter offer this warning to his readers here? How is it applicable today?

2. Choose one verse or phrase from 1 Peter 5 that stands out to you. This could be something you're intrigued by, something that makes you uncomfortable, something that puzzles you, something that resonates with you, or just something you want to examine further. Write that here.

Going Deeper

From the Commentary

> The image of the flock is often used in the Bible, and it is a very instructive one (see Ps. 23; 100; Isa. 40:11; Luke 15:4–6; John 10; Acts 20:28; Heb. 13:20–21; 1 Peter 2:25; Rev. 7:17). We were once stray sheep, wandering toward ruin, but the Good Shepherd found us and restored us to the fold.
>
> Sheep are clean animals, unlike dogs and pigs (2 Peter 2:20–22). Sheep tend to flock together, and God's people need to be together. Sheep are notoriously ignorant and prone to wander away if they do not follow the shepherd. Sheep are defenseless, for the most part, and need their shepherd to protect them (Ps. 23:4).
>
> Sheep are very useful animals. Jewish shepherds tended their sheep, not for the meat (which would have been costly) but for the wool, milk, and lambs. God's people should be useful to Him and certainly ought to "reproduce" themselves by bringing others to Christ. Sheep were used for the sacrifices, and we ought to be "living sacrifices," doing the will of God (Rom. 12:1–2).
>
> *—Be Hopeful*, pages 143–44

3. What does it mean to be a shepherd leader? What responsibilities did Peter remind shepherd leaders that they have? (See 1 Peter 5:1–3.)

From the Commentary

Since this is the epistle of hope, Peter brought in once again the promise of the Lord's return. His coming is an encouragement in suffering (1 Peter 1:7–8) and a motivation for faithful service. If a pastor ministers to please himself or to please people, he will have a disappointing and difficult ministry. "It must be hard to keep all these people happy," a visitor said to me after a church service. "I don't even try to keep them happy," I replied with a smile. "I try to please the Lord, and I let Him take care of the rest."

Jesus Christ is the *Good* Shepherd who died for the sheep (John 10:11), the *Great* Shepherd who lives for the sheep (Heb. 13:20–21), and the *Chief* Shepherd who comes for the sheep (1 Peter 5:4). As the Chief Shepherd, He alone can assess a man's ministry and give him the proper reward. Some who appear to be first may end up last when the Lord examines each man's ministry.

—*Be Hopeful*, page 148

4. What is the "crown of glory that will never fade away" (1 Peter 5:4)? What does it take to earn this crown?

From Today's World

There have always been good and bad leaders in our world. History reports stories of both kinds—from the worst possible kind to the best. In today's world, leaders still take on all shapes and sizes. Some quietly go about their work in the local church while others build huge platforms from which they teach their wisdom through books, seminars, and even television shows. The motivation for leaders varies as much as they do. Some lead because they are gifted with leadership and called to use that gift. Others decide they want to be leaders in order to gain influence and wealth.

5. What is the test of a true leader? In what ways do some people put the cart before the horse as they seek to become leaders? How do you know when someone is leading according to godly principles? How do you know when they're motivated by the pursuit of worldly success? What advice would Peter give today's leaders?

From the Commentary

Peter had already admonished the saints to be submissive to government authorities (1 Peter 2:13–17), the slaves to submit to their masters (1 Peter 2:18–25), and the wives to their husbands (1 Peter 3:1–7). Now he commanded all of the believers to submit to God and to each other.

The younger believers should submit to the older believers, not only out of respect for their age, but also out of respect for their spiritual maturity.

—*Be Hopeful,* pages 153–54

6. Review 1 Peter 5:5–7. Why do you suppose Peter singled out younger believers in these verses? What do older believers bring to the table that younger believers can't? What can the modern church learn from this admonishment?

From the Commentary

According to 1 Peter 5:7, we must *once and for all* give all of our cares— past, present, and future—to the Lord. We must not hand them to Him piecemeal, keeping those cares that we think we can handle ourselves. If we keep "the little cares" for ourselves, they will soon become big problems! Each time a new burden arises, we must by faith remind the Lord (and ourselves) that we have already turned it over to Him.

If anybody knew from experience that God cares for His own, it was Peter! When you read the four gospels, you discover that Peter shared in some wonderful miracles.

—*Be Hopeful,* page 155

7. Read Mark 1:29–31; Luke 5:1–11; Matthew 17:24–27; Matthew 14:22–33; Luke 22:50–51 (with John 18:10–11); and Acts 12. What do these passages reveal about God's care for Peter? What does this teach us about God's care for His people?

From the Commentary

One reason we have cares is because we have an enemy. As the serpent, Satan deceives (2 Cor. 11:3), and as the lion, Satan devours. The word *Satan* means "adversary," and the word *devil* means "the accuser, the slanderer." The recipients of this letter had already experienced the attacks of the slanderer (1 Peter 4:4, 14), and now they would meet "the lion" in their fiery trial. Peter gave them several practical instructions to help them get victory over their adversary.

—*Be Hopeful,* page 156

8. Review 1 Peter 5:8–9. What instructions did Peter give about preparing to deal with Satan? (See also John 8:44; 2 Cor. 11:13–15.) How is this advice applicable to Christians today?

More to Consider: Read James 4:7. How is this message similar to the one Peter gave in 1 Peter 5:8–9?

From the Commentary

Peter closed on a positive note and reminded his readers that God knew what He was doing and was in complete control. No matter how difficult the fiery trial may become, a Christian always has hope. Peter gave several reasons for this hopeful attitude.

We have God's grace. Our salvation is because of His grace (1 Peter 1:10). He called us before we called on Him (1 Peter 1:2). We have "tasted that the Lord is gracious" (1 Peter 2:3), so we are not afraid of anything that He purposes for us. His grace is "manifold" (1 Peter 4:10) and meets every situation of life. As we submit to Him, He gives us the grace that we need. In fact, He is "the God of all grace." He has grace to help in every time of need (Heb. 4:16). "He giveth more grace" (James 4:6), and we must stand in that grace (1 Peter 5:12; see Rom. 5:2).

We know we are going to glory. He has "called us unto his eternal glory by Christ Jesus." This is the wonderful inheritance into which we were born (1 Peter 1:4). Whatever begins with God's grace will always lead to God's glory (Ps. 84:11).

Our present suffering is only for a while. Our various trials are only "for a season" (1 Peter 1:6), but the glory that results is *eternal*.

We know that our trials are building Christian character.... God has several tools that He uses to equip His people for life and service, and suffering is one of them. The Word of God is another tool (2 Tim. 3:16–17, where "thoroughly furnished" means "fully equipped"). He also uses the fellowship and ministry of the church (Eph. 4:11–16). Our Savior in heaven is perfecting His children so that they will do His will and His work (Heb. 13:20–21).

—*Be Hopeful*, pages 158–59

9. How would the early Christians have received Peter's message of hope? Why is encouragement such as this important for believers? How do we find similar encouragement today?

From the Commentary

> Paul always ended his letters with a benediction of grace (2 Thess. 3:17–18). Peter closed this epistle with a benediction of peace. He opened the letter with a greeting of peace (1 Peter 1:2), so the entire epistle points to "God's peace" from beginning to end. What a wonderful way to end a letter that announced the coming of a fiery trial!
>
> —*Be Hopeful,* page 160

10. Why is it significant that Peter opened and closed with the theme of peace? What sort of peace did the early Christians seek? What peace do we seek today? How might our Christian communities be different if we earnestly sought Christ's peace?

Looking Inward

Take a moment to reflect on all that you've explored thus far in this study of 1 Peter 5. Review your notes and answers and think about how each of these things matters in your life today.

Tips for Small Groups: To get the most out of this section, form pairs or trios and have group members take turns answering these questions. Be honest and as open as you can in this discussion, but most of all, be encouraging and supportive of others. Be sensitive to those who are going through particularly difficult times and don't press for people to speak if they're uncomfortable doing so.

11. Are you, or have you ever been, a leader? What sort of leader are you? How does Peter's message about shepherd leaders relate to your leadership role? What can you learn from this to help you be a better leader?

12. In what ways are you a good example to other believers? Why is this important? What are some ways you aren't such a great example? How can you work on these things?

13. The Bible reveals many ways God cared for Peter. What are some of the ways you've seen God's hand in your life? Have you ever experienced something you would call a miracle? Explain. How important is it for you to trust that God is caring for you in supernatural ways?

Going Forward

14. Think of one or two things that you have learned that you'd like to work on in the coming week. Remember that this is all about quality, not quantity. It's better to work on one specific area of life and do it well than to work on many and do poorly (or to be so overwhelmed that you simply don't try).

Do you want to learn more about how to be a shepherd leader? Be specific. Go back through 1 Peter 5 and put a star next to the phrase or verse that is most encouraging to you. Consider memorizing this verse.

Real-Life Application Ideas: Since "hope" is Peter's overarching theme in this letter, take time to consider what it means to share hope with someone. Then think about ways you can be a hope giver to another. Perhaps you have a friend or family member who's hungry for encouragement. Make a plan for providing hope to that person in the coming weeks. For example, this could include such things as emails, letters, taking the person to lunch, and praying with him or her.

Seeking Help

15. Write a prayer below (or simply pray one in silence), inviting God to work on your mind and heart in those areas you've noted above. Be honest about your desires and fears.

Notes for Small Groups:
- *Look for ways to put into practice the things you wrote in the Going Forward section. Talk with other group members about your ideas and commit to being accountable to one another.*
- *During the coming week, ask the Holy Spirit to continue to reveal truth to you from what you've read and studied.*

5/23/19

C's grandson graduated
Joh Hopkins
S dealing w/ teenage son
K's office dealing
L's husband's travels
D's retirement

Summary and Review

Notes for Small Groups: This session is a summary and review of this book. Because of that, it is shorter than the previous lessons. If you are using this in a small-group setting, consider combining this lesson with a time of fellowship or a shared meal.

> *Before you begin...*
> - *Pray for the Holy Spirit to reveal truth and wisdom as you go through this lesson.*
> - *Briefly review the notes you made in the previous sessions. You will refer back to previous sections throughout this bonus lesson.*

Looking Back

1. Over the past eight lessons, you've examined 1 Peter. What expectations did you bring to this study? In what ways were those expectations met?

2. What is the most significant personal discovery you've made from this study?

3. What surprised you most about Peter's message of hope? What, if anything, troubled you?

Progress Report

4. Take a few moments to review the Going Forward sections of the previous lessons. How would you rate your progress for each of the things you chose to work on? What adjustments, if any, do you need to make to continue on the path toward spiritual maturity?

5. In what ways have you grown closer to Christ during this study? Take a moment to celebrate those things. Then think of areas where you feel you still need to grow and note those here. Make plans to revisit this study in a few weeks to review your growing faith.

Things to Pray About

6. First Peter is a book celebrating Jesus' victory on the cross and the hope we have in Christ. As you reflect on this life-changing message, consider how it changes the way you live your life and the way you reach out to those who don't yet know this truth.

7. The messages in 1 Peter include hope, growing through suffering, submission, and learning to lead with humility. Spend time praying for each of these topics.

8. Whether you've been studying this in a small group or on your own, there are many other Christians working through the very same issues you discovered when examining 1 Peter. Take time to pray for them, that God would reveal truth, that the Holy Spirit would guide you, and that each person might grow in spiritual maturity according to God's will.

A Blessing of Encouragement

Studying the Bible is one of the best ways to learn how to be more like Christ. Thanks for taking this step. In closing, let this blessing precede you and follow you into the next week while you continue to marinate in God's Word:

May God light your path to greater understanding as you review the truths found in 1 Peter and consider how they can help you grow closer to Christ.